Acknowledgement of Land & of the Traditional Owners of this Land

I would like to acknowledge the Gadigal people of the Eora Nation, upon whose stolen land I stand on today.
I recognise that this land was never terra nullius — the land belonging to these peoples was never ceded, given up, bought or sold.
I would like to pay my respects to Aboriginal Elders past, present and emerging, and I extend this acknowledgement to all Aboriginal and Torres Strait Islander people.

Eve Of Destruction

"The Eastern world, it is explodin'
Violence flarin', bullets loadin'
You're old enough to kill but not for votin'
You don't believe in war, but what's that gun you're totin'?
And even the Jordan river has bodies floatin'.

But you tell me over and over and over again my friend
Ah, you don't believe we're on the eve of destruction.

Don't you understand what I'm trying to say?
Can't you feel the fear that I'm feeling today?
If the button is pushed, there's no running away
There'll be no one to save with the world in a grave
Take a look around you boy, it's bound to scare you, boy.

But you tell me over and over and over again, my friend
Ah, you don't believe we're on the eve of destruction.

Yeah, my blood's so mad, feels like coagulatin'
I'm sittin' here just contemplatin'
I can't twist the truth, it knows no regulation
Handful of Senators don't pass legislation.

And marches alone can't bring integration
When human respect is disintegratin'
This whole crazy world is just too frustratin'.

And you tell me over and over and over again my friend
Ah, you don't believe we're on the eve of destruction."

"Think of all the hate there is in Red China
Then take a look around to Selma, Alabama
Ah, you may leave here for four days in space
But when you return, it's the same old place
The poundin' of the drums, the pride and disgrace
You can bury your dead but don't leave a trace
Hate your nextdoor neighbour but don't forget to say grace.

And you tell me over and over and over and over again my friend
You don't believe we're on the eve of destruction.

You don't believe we're on the eve of destruction."

Songwriters: Barri Steve/Sloan PF
Performed by: Barry McGuire

Preet Kaur Nanak
(Insta: preekaurnanak)

Preet Kaur Nanak
(Insta: preekaurnanak)

Preet Kaur Nanak
(Insta: preekaurnanak)

CONTENTS

1: I'm a Disgusting Person
(Sono Una Persona Disgustosa)
2: I Was Doing Everything Wrong!
(Stavo Facendo Tutto Sbagliato)
3: What Would Have Happened If...?
(Che Cosa Sarebbe Successo Se...?)
4: Get FUCKED!
(Fatti SCOPARE!)
5: Attraction
(Attrazione)
6: War Machine
(Macchina da Guerra)
7: Peace Machine
(Macchina della Pace)
8: Wait in Line
(Aspettate in Fila)
9: Fuck This Shit
(A Va Fanculo Questa Merda)
10: "Mummy, I See Dead People Everywhere!"
("Mamma, Vedo Morti Ovunque!")
11: Don't Be Scared!
(Non Aver Paura!)
12: Let Your Hair Grow
(Lascia che i tuoi Capelli Crescano)
13: The Mind's Eye
(L'occhio della Mente)
14: I'm Not Gonna Run Away
(Non Scapperò Via)
15: Curiosity Did Not Kill the Kat
(La Curiosità non ha Ucciso il Kat)
16: Values
(Valori)
17: Virago
18: Corrupt:Corruption
(Corrotto:Corruzione)

CONTENTS

19: Find What You LO♥E & Let it Kill You
(Trova Ciò che Ami e Lascia che ti Uccida)
20: Believe in Yourself
(Credi in te Stesso)
21: Open Your Eyes
(Apri gli Occhi)
22: Do Not Think!
(Non Pensare!)
23: Women Will Rule the World
(Le Donne Domineranno il Mondo)
24: Is Money Evil?
(è il Denaro Male?)
25: Stupidity
(Stupidità)
26: Greed
(Avidità)
27: I Walk Alone!
(Io Cammina da Solo!)
28: Ship of Fools
(La Nave dei Folli)
29: Don't Play It Safe!
(Non Giocare sul Sicuro!)
30: Be a Rebel!
(Sii un Ribelle!)
31: How Can You?
(Come Puoi?)
32: Bright Eyes
(Occhi Vivaci)
33: Religion
(Religione)
34: Den of Iniquity
(Luogo dell'iniquità)
35: Born to be Wild
(Nato per essere Selvaggio)

CONTENTS

36: Hack the System
(Hackera il Sistema)
37: Actions Speak Louder than Words
(Le Azioni Parlano più Forte delle Parole)
38: Never Stop
(Mai Smettere)
39: Heaven, Hell & Earth
(Paradiso, Inferno e Terra)
40: I Walk with Others
(Cammino con gli Altri)
41: Which Life?
(Quale Vita?)
42: The Men Who Sold the Earth
(Gli Uomini che hanno Venduto la Terra)
43: Don't Let the Music Stop
(Non Lasciare che la Musica si Fermi)
44: Altered Consciousness
(Coscienza alterata)
45: Reforest the Amazon!
(Rimboschire l'Amazzonia!)
46: Easy Prey
(Preda Facile)
47: In Search for the Meaning of Life
(Alla Ricerca del Senso della Vita)
48: Be a Warrior
(Essere un Guerriero)
49: May All Your Dreams Come True
(Possano tutti i tuoi Sogni Avverarsi)
50: The Future
(Il Futuro)

I'm a Disgusting Person
(Sono Una Persona Disgustosa)

I don't wash my *"keep cup"*.
I don't wash my sheets.
I don't wash the dishes.
I don't wash the floors.
I don't wash myself.
I'm a disgusting person.

I do disgusting things.
I think disgusting thoughts.
I have disgusting feelings.
I smell disgusting.
I look disgusting.
I'm a disgusting person.

I don't use *"Eude Colone"*.
I don't wash myself.
I don't comb my hair.
I don't shave.
I don't smile.
I'm a disgusting person.

I smell.
I smell of *"B.O."*.
I fart a lot.
I swear a lot.
I use foul language.
I use words like...
...fuck.
...pussy.
...arsehole.
...cock.
...shit.
I'm a disgusting person.

"So, you'd better stay away from me because...
... I'm a disgusting person."

"The Don"
14.10.2021

I Was Doing Everything Wrong!
(Stavo Facendo Tutto Sbagliato)

I was not doing it right.
I had miscalculated.
I was using the wrong strategy.
I was using the wrong approach.
I was using the wrong methodology.
I was doing everything wrong!

Do not touch.
Do not speak.
Do not make people feel uncomfortable.
Do not be too intense.
Do not make the first move.
This is why...
...I was doing everything wrong!

Be cool.
Be calm.
Be relaxed.
Be sensitive.
Be friendly.
Be non-judgemental.
I was doing everything wrong!

Let them make the first move.
Let them control.
Let them have the power.
Let them do whatever they want.
Let them *"Be"*.
I was doing everything wrong!

"Definitely, do not tell her you LO♥E her!"

"The Don"
14.10.2021

What Would Have Happened If...?
(Che Cosa Sarebbe Successo Se...?)

What would have happened if...
...Bob Dylan had not gone to New York?
What would have happened if...
...JFK had not been shot?
What would have happened if...
...Martin Luther king had not been shot?
What would have happened if...
...Robert Kennedy had not been shot?
What would have happened if...
...Jimi Hendrix had not overdosed?
What would have happened if...
...Jim Morrison had not overdosed?
What would have happened if...
...Janis Joplin had not died of an overdose?
What would have happened if...
...Gough Whitlam had not been kicked out of office?
What would have happened if...
...John Lennon had not been murdered?
What would have happened if...
...Amy Winehouse had not died of an overdose?
What would have happened if...
...if you had not been born?
What would have happened if...
...if I had not been born?

"How would the world be different?"

What would have happened if...

What would have happened if...

What would have happened if...

What would have happened if...

"The Don"
14.10.2021

GET FUCKED!

(Fatti SCOPARE!)

Fuck YOU!

Get FUCKED!

"The Don"
14.10.2021

Attraction

(Attrazione)

What makes a person attractive?
Is it looks?
Is it chemistry?
Is it intellectual?
Is emotional?
Is it spiritual?
Is it lust?
Is it passion?
Is it fate?
Is it destiny?
Is it the Universe?
Is it something unexplainable?
What makes someone attractive?

I've never fathomed it out.
I've never figured it out.
I've never worked it out.
I've never understood it.
I've always tried to work it out.
What makes someone attractive?

Is it written in the stars?

Is it just perception?

What is the answer to that unanswerable question?
What is attraction?

Attraction is the name of the game.

Maybe!

"The Don"
16.10.2021

WAR MACHINE

(Macchina da Guerra)

The War Machine *is in control.*
The War Machine *has the power.*
The War Machine *makes decisions.*
The War Machine *has no morals.*
The War Machine *has no ethics.*
The War Machine *has no conscience.*
The War Machine *takes no prisoners.*
The War Machine *shows no sympathy.*
The War Machine *takes no sides.*
The War Machine *is built to kill.*
The War Machine *is built to destroy.*
The War Machine *is built to make money.*
The War Machine *is built by the "Military Industrial Complex".*
The War Machine *is built for wars.*
The War Machine *creates conflicts.*
The War Machine *creates wars.*
The War Machine *LO❤ES wars.*
The War Machine *builds all the guns, tanks, planes, bombs to kill & destroy.*
The War Machine *creates conflicts & wars to sell its merchandise of death & destruction.*
The War Machine *sells its products of doom for money...*
...for profits.
The War Machine *is controlled by a small group of men.*
The War Machine *is insatiable.*
The War Machine *cannot be stopped.*
The War Machine *is not intelligent.*
The War Machine *will destroy the planet.*
And in so doing...
...will destroy itself.

But it will be too late!

Everything will have been destroyed by "The War Machine"!

"The Don"
17.10.2021

Peace Machine

(Macchina della Pace)

It's *"Good"* verses *"Evil"*.
It's a titanic battle.
It's the battle for the planet.
It's the battle for humanity.
It's the battle for survival.
It's the battle for existence.
It's a *"David verses Goliath"* battle.
It's the battle between *"War"* & *"Peace"*.
It's the battle between money verses spirituality.
It's the battle between greed verses kindness.
It's the battle between the mighty, unscrupulous *"War Machine"* & the moral & ethical, *"Peace Machine"*.
It's the battle between *"Capitalism"* & *"profits"* against *"Humanity"* & *"valuing ALL forms of LIFE"*.

The *"War Machine"* has the upper hand at the moment.
But the war is not over yet.
Can the *"Peace Machine"* make a comeback?
Does it have the stamina?
Does it have the *"willpower"*?

In the end there is no alternative.
The *"Peace Machine"* has to win!
Otherwise, we are all destroyed!

"The Don"
17.10.2021

Wait in Line

(Aspettate in Fila)

What's your hurry?
Take it easy.
Take it slow.
Take your time.
Be cool.
Don't rush.
Enjoy the ride.
But…
…*wait in line.*

She'll let you know when she's ready.
It's all up to her.
She decides.
She's in no rush.
She has a vibrator.
She doesn't need you.
So...
... *wait in line.*

Until she's ready.
Maybe she'll never be ready...
... for you!
You might have to wait a very long time.
But however long it takes.
You must...
... *wait in line.*

"The Don"
17.10.2021

FUCK THIS SHIT

(A Va Fanculo Questa Merda)

We have become objects.
We have become machines.
We have become commodities.
We have become *"things"*!
We have become dehumanised.
I hate this shit.
Fuck this shit.

We are manipulated.
We are programmed.
We are abused.
We are told what to do...
...and when to do it...
... and whom to do it with.
We have become dehumanised.
I hate this shit.
Fuck this shit.

We are not allowed to see.
We are not allowed to hear.
We are not allowed to feel.
We are not allowed to think.
We are not allowed to be ourselves.
We are not allowed to grow!
We are not allowed to LIVE.
We are not allowed to LO♥E!
We have become dehumanised.
I hate this shit.
Fuck this shit.

"The Don" & Miriam
18.10.2021

"Mummy, I See Dead People Everywhere!"
("Mamma, Vedo Morti Ovunque!")

"Mummy, I see dead people everywhere!"
"Yes dear, they are the walking dead!"
People that have no curiosity.
People that have no interests.
People that have no creativity.
People that have no life.

"Mummy, I see dead people everywhere!"
"Yes dear, they are the walking dead!"
People that have no eyes.
People that have no ears.
People that have no minds.

"Mummy, I see dead people everywhere!"
"Yes dear, they are the walking dead!"
People that have no feelings.
People that have no heart.
People that have no souls.
People that are dead.

"Mummy, I see dead people everywhere!"

"Mummy, I see dead people everywhere!"

"Mummy, I see dead people everywhere!"

"Mummy, I see dead people everywhere!"

"The Don"
19.10.2021

Don't Be Scared!

(Non Aver Paura!)

Are you scared?
Are you afraid?
Are you prepared to take your mask off?
Are you ready to reveal yourself?
It's time.
Don't be scared!

Say what you think.
Do what you feel.
Go where you want to go.
Be who you want to be.
It's time.
Don't be scared!

Do be afraid!
Don't be nervous.
Don't be cautious.
Don't be inhibited.
It's time.
Don't be scared!

Shout it out loud.
Say what you want to say.
Let everyone hear it.
Do be afraid to speak your mind.
It's time.
Don't be scared!

"The Don"
20.10.2021

Let Your Hair Grow

(Lascia che i tuoi Capelli Crescano)

Buck the trend.
Go against the fashion.
Swim against the tide.
Go feral.
Go *"natural"*.
Let your hair grow...
...long!

Don't shave your head.
Don't cut your hair.
Don't be a *"follower of fashion"*.
Make a stand against conservatism.
Make a stand against *"Fascism"*.
Let your locks grow freely.
Let nature take its course.
Let your hair grow...
...long!

Take back your head.
Reclaim your hair.
Let's go back to the '60s & 70s.
Back to a time when we spoke of *"make LO♥E not war"*.
A time of *"Hippies"*, *"Flower Power"* & *"Flower Children"*.
A time of *"Psychedelia"*, *"Counterculture"* & *"LSD"*.
A time when hair was considered beautiful.
Very long hair.
Shoulder length hair.
Waist length hair.
When a metre wide *"fro"* was considered *"COOL"*.
Let's bring back hair.
Let your hair grow...
...long!

Set a trend.
Be a *"trend setter"*.
Buck the *"style police"*.
Buck the *"System"*.
Set your own style.
Follow your own fashion.
Write your own rules.
Set an example.
Start the trend.
Pave the way.
Be a leader.
Others will follow.
Let your hair grow...
...long!

"The Don"
20.10.2021

The Mind's Eye

(L'occhio della Mente)

Can you see?
Maybe it's the *"3rd Eye"*?
Maybe it's the *"2 1/2"* eye?
Maybe it's the *"no"* eye?
Maybe you are blind?
Maybe you can see without eyes?
Do you have *"The Mind's Eye"*?

What can you see?
Can you see things that others cannot?
Can you see the *"unseen"*?
Can you see *"The Light"*?
Can you see *"The Force"*?
Can you see the *"Walking Dead"*?
Can you see with your *"Mind's Eye"*?

What can you see?
Can you see the hatred?
Can you see the violence?
Can you see the abuse?
Can you see the exploitation?
Can you see the discrimination?
Can you see the cruelty?
Can you see the inhumanity?

What can you see?
Can you see BEAUTY?
Can you see INNOCENCE?
Can you see COMPASSION?
Can you see RESPECT?
Can you see FREEDOM?
Can you see LO♥E?

If you can...
...you are seeing with your *"Mind's Eye"*!

The *"Mind's Eye"* sees what your physical eyes cannot!
What can you see?

"The Don"
23.10.2021

I'm Not Gonna Run Away
(Non Scapperò Via)

I've done my share of running.
I'm gonna stop.
I'm gonna stand my ground.
I'm not gonna run away...
...this time!

I've had enough of running.
I've had enough of fleeing.
I've had enough of being a coward.
I'm not gonna run away...
...not anymore.

It's time to make a stand.
It's time to hold my ground.
It's time to be strong.
I'm not gonna run away...
... never again!

I'm not gonna run away!

"The Don"
23.10.2021

Curiosity Did Not Kill the Kat

(La Curiosità non ha Ucciso il Kat)

Curiosity did not kill the Kat.
Society killed the Kat.
She was asking too many questions.
She was causing troubles.
She was inspiring others to think.
She was starting a *"Movement"*.
The *"Be Curious"* movement.
She had to be stopped.
This could not be allowed to continue.
So, she was silenced.
She was removed.
She was taken out.
She was taken down.
Curiosity did not kill the Kat.
Society killed the Kat.

She was an insurgent.
She was subversive.
She was a trouble-maker.
She was causing unrest.
She was starting a rebellion.
She was starting a revolution.
She was becoming a leader.
She was getting followers.
She was starting a *"Movement"*.
The *"Be Curious"* movement.
She had to be stopped.
This could not be allowed to continue.
So, she was silenced.
She was removed.
She was taken out.
She was taken down.
Curiosity did not kill the Kat.
Society killed the Kat.
Curiosity is not to blame.
Curiosity is innocent.
Curiosity has been framed!
Curiosity did not kill the Kat.
Society killed the Kat!

"The Don"
25.10.2021

Values

(Valori)

What are your values?
What are your principles?
What are your *"Life Rules"*?
What do *"stand for"*?
What is your *"moral compass"*?
So...
...what are your values?

Do they include...
...respect?
...compassion?
...friendship?
...kindness?
...human rights?
...equal rights?
...egalitarianism?
...humanity?
...LO♥E?

If they do...
...then you're a friend of mine.

Will you ever compromise these values?
Have you ever compromised these values?
Have you ever *"sold"* them out?
Do your *"values"* have a price?
How much will you sell them for?
What price do put on your values?

If you do not sell your values...
If your values are priceless...
...then you're a friend of mine.

What are your Values?
Are you a friend of mine?

"The Don"
25.10.2021

Virago

Are you a warrior?
Are you a fighter?
Are you a battler?
Are you an *"Amazonian"*?
Are you a *"Viking Queen"*?
Are you a "Virago"?

Are you a woman of strength?
Are you a woman of power?
Are you a woman of fortitude?
Are you a woman of *"Lesbos"*?
Are you a woman warrior?
Are you a "Virago"?

Are you a woman that takes shit from no one?
Are you a woman that challenges the male domination?
Are you a woman that challenges the *"Patriarchy"*?
Are you a woman that wants to change the *"System"*?
Are you a woman that wants to bring down *"The Establishment"*?
Are you a woman that wants a revolution?
Are you a woman rebel?
Are you a *"wild"* woman?
Are you a "Virago"?

"The Don"
25.10.2021

Corrupt:Corruption

(Corrotto:Corruzione)

What is corruption?
Corruption for me is selling your values & principles for personal gain.
It's more to do with...
..."moral" corruption.
..."ethical" corruption.
Selling out one's values.
Betraying one's own "core beliefs".
Rather than legal corruption.

Are you corrupt?
I don't believe so.
I don't think I have ever sold myself.

Do you have a price?
Would you ever sell yourself...
... just for personal gain?
I'd like to think that I wouldn't.
But...
...one never really knows.
There is always temptation.
Maybe...
...my price is set very high.
...& no one has reached it yet.

Do you think most people are corrupt?
Yes!
Unfortunately, I do!

How about you?
Are you corrupt?
Do you have a price?

"The Don"
26.10.2021

Find What You LO♥E & Let it Kill You
(Trova Ciò che Ami e Lascia che ti Uccida)

Let it swallow you up.
Let yourself be engulfed by it.
Let it consume you.
Let yourself be subsumed by it.
Let it envelope you.
Let it surround you.
Let it dominate you.
Let it control you.
Let it overpower you.
Let it suffocate you.
Let it devour you.
Let it eat you.
Let it satiate you.
Let it destroy you.
Let it annihilate you.
Let it kill you.

Find what you LO♥E & let it kill you!

So that you can be *"Reborn"*.
So that you can arise like a phoenix from its ashes.
So that you become a new *"Being"*.

So...
...Find what you LO♥E & let it kill you!

"The Don"
26.10.2021

Believe in Yourself

(Credi in te Stesso)

Don't doubt yourself.
Don't put yourself down.
Don't be hard on yourself.
Don't punish yourself.
Don't be unkind to yourself.
Believe in yourself.

Be kind to yourself.
Be easy on yourself.
Be gentle to yourself.
Be friendly to yourself.
Be LO♥ING to yourself.
Believe in yourself.

Believe that you are unique.
Believe that you are beautiful.
Beautiful that you are awesome.
Believe that you are important.
Believe that you are amazing.
Believe in yourself.

LO♥E yourself.

Believe in yourself.

"The Don"
26.10.2021

Open Your Eyes

(Apri gli Occhi)

Look around you.
What do you see?
Are you really looking?
Are you really seeing?
Are you seeing what is around you?
Can you see *what you are not supposed to see?*
Can you see *what you are not allowed to see?*
Open your eues!

Can you see the *lies?*
Can you see the *propaganda?*
Can you see the *façade?*
Can you see the *veneer?*
Can you see the *illusion?*
Can you see the *"bullshit"?*
Can you see the *fakeness?*
Can you see the *hypocrisy?*
Can you see the *hatred?*
Can you see the *"Fool's Gold"?*
Can you see the *tricks?*
Can you see the *horror?*
Can you see the *pain?*
Can you see the *suffering?*
Can you see the *torment?*
Can you see the *inhumanity?*

If you can't...
...open your eyes!

See!
Open your eyes!
Don't be blind.
Open your eyes!

"The Don"
26.10.2021

Do Not Think!

(Non Pensare!)

Do not think.
Get rid of the noise.
Do not think!

Thinking is bad for you.
Thinking causes problems for you.
Do not think!

Have nothing in your mind.
Let your mind be empty.
Do not think!

Clear yourself of all thoughts.
Remove your thoughts.
Do not think!

Make you mind be at peace.
Let you mind be still.
Do not think!

Let your mind be free.
Let your mind fly.
Do not think!

Let your mind sour into the sky.
Let your mind get *"High"*.
Do not think!

Do not think!

Do not think!

Do not think!

Do not think!

"The Don"
26.10.2021

Women Will Rule the World

(Le Donne Domineranno il Mondo)

It's only a matter of time.
Women will rule the world.
Women will take over the reins of power.
Women will rule the world.
It's only a matter of time.
Women will rule the world.

Women are more intelligent than men.
Women are more sensitive than men
It's only a matter of time.
Women will rule the world.

Women are more caring than men.
Women are more mature than men.
It's only a matter of time.
Women will rule the world.

Women are more skilful than men.
Women are kinder than men.
It's only a matter of time.
Women will rule the world.

Women are smarter than men.
Women are wiser than men.
It's only a matter of time.
Women will rule the world.

Women are more fearless than men.
Women are braver than men.
It's only a matter of time.
Women will rule the world.

Women are more resilient than men.
It's only a matter of time.
Women will rule the world.

It's only a matter of time.
Women will rule the world.

"The Don"
26.10.2021

Is Money Evil?
(è il Denaro Male?)

Is money really evil?
What would happen if we didn't have money?
Would society be any different?
How would it be different?
What sort of *"System"* could replace it?
Is it even imaginable?
Is money evil?

There would be no commerce.
There would be no accountants.
There would be no economists.
There would be no *"Economic Theory"*.
There would be no banks.
There would be no profits.
There would be no *"Capitalism"*.
Is that even possible?
Is money evil?

Is money really evil?
What would happen if we didn't have money?
Would greed still exist?
Would the notion of *"unlimited acquisition"* still exist?
Would humans have other values in its place?
Would we have different priorities?
What could these be?
If money no longer existed.
Because...
... money is evil!

"Can I borrow a couple of dollars?"
"I'll pay you back tomorrow!"
"I promise!"

"The Don"
27.10.2021

Stupidity

(Stupidità)

Stupidity is rampant.
Stupidity is endemic.
Stupidity is systemic.
Stupidity is pervasive.
Stupidity is insidious.
Stupidity is poisonous.
Stupidity is lunacy.
Stupidity is EVERYWHERE.

Stupidity is in the air that we breathe.
Stupidity is in the food we eat.
Stupidity is in the water we drink.
Stupidity is in the newspapers we read.
Stupidity is in the politicians.
Stupidity is in the churches
Stupidity is in society.
Stupidity is in our minds.
Stupidity is in our thoughts.
Stupidity is in our imagination.
Stupidity is our *"Being"*.
Stupidity is in us.
Stupidity is in me.
Stupidity is EVERYWHERE.

We are ALL stupid!

"The Don"
27.10.2021

Greed

(Avidità)

What is *"Greed"*?
Why are we greedy?
Is it built into our DNA?
Why do we want more than what we need?
Why do we want to accumulate more & more?
Why are we so greedy?
Can we ever get rid of greed?

Don't be greedy, there is more than enough for everyone.
You don't need more than what is required.
"Sharing is caring!"
There is no need for greed!

Greed is unnecessary!
Greed is illogical!
Greed is stupid!
Greed is BAD!

Let's get rid of greed!

We don't need it!

"The Don"
28.10.2021

I Walk Alone!

(Io Cammina da Solo!)

I don't need your help.
I don't need your support.
I can stand on my own two feet.
I don't need anyone.
I don't need you.
I walk alone!

I am a woman.
I am strong.
I am independent.
I am powerful.
I don't need a man.
I walk alone!

I don't need your help.
I don't need you to walk me home.
I walk alone!

I walk alone!

I walk alone!

I walk alone!

"The Don"
29.10.2021

Ship of Fools

(La Nave dei Folli)

We are all fools?
Can't we see what's happening?
Can't we see what's around us?
Can't we see?
Are we blind?
Are we just fools?
Are we sailing in a "Ship of Fools"?

Who is the captain?
Where is the captain?
Who is the crew?
Are we the crew?
I think I'm on a "Ship of Fools"?

This ship has no direction.
It is sailing aimlessly on the sea.
It has lost its way.
But those on the ship don't know it.
It is a "Ship of Fools"!

They have no idea that they are lost.
Lost at sea.
They are delusional.
They are completely mindless beings.
They are on the "Ship of Fools".

Look around you.
Do you know where you are?
Do you know who you're with?
Do you know where you're going?
Maybe...
...you too are on that "Ship of Fools"!

Are you a fool?

"The Don"
29.10.2021

Don't Play It Safe!

(Non Giocare sul Sicuro!)

Don't conform.
Don't worry about what other people think.
Don't worry about being *"Judged"*.
Don't be one of the *"Walking Dead"*.
Don't be a *"Zombie"*.
Don't be *"Lifeless"*.
Don't play it safe!

Breakout of your *"Comfort Zone"*.
Express yourself.
Be free to be whomever you want to be.
Be free to do whatever you want to do.
Be free to do it with whomever you want.
Be alive.
Be creative.
Don't play it safe!

Take risks.
Take chances.
Take control.
Take charge.
Take your life back.
Don't play it safe!

Have adventures.
Have excitement.
Have fun.
Have positivity.
Have optimism.
Don't play it safe!

"The Don"
29.10.2021

Be a Rebel!

(Sii un Ribelle!)

Do not conform.
Be an individual.
Be unique.
Be yourself.
Be eccentric.
Be weird.
Be a rebel!

Do not follow the crowd.
Do not follow trends.
Do not follow fashions.
Do not follow the sheep.
Do not follow the *"Establishment"*
Do not follow anyone.
Be a rebel!

Be rebellious.
Be a radical.
Be a revolutionary.
Be a *"Freedom Fighter".*
Be an agitator.
Be a *"Polemicist".*
Be a rebel!

"Sappho" was a rebel.
"Hypatia" was a rebel.
"Emmeline Pankhurst" was a rebel too.
"Che Guevara" was a rebel.
"Martin Luther King" was a rebel.
"Julian Assange" is a rebel.
"Chelsea Manning" is a rebel.
"Edward Snowden" is a rebel.

"Are you a rebel too?"
"Rebel, rebel, rebel, rebel!"

"The Don"
30.10.2021

How Can You?
(Come Puoi?)

How can stand & watch all the violence around you?
How can you stand & watch all the injustice in world?
How can you stand & watch all the inhumanity in society?
How can you stand & watch all the death in this world?
How can you stand, watch & do nothing?
How can you?

How can you sit in your comfy lounge & watch people starving?
How can you sleep in you comfortable bed knowing that others sleep in the rain?
How can you eat your nutritious food knowing other people have no food to eat?
How can you live in your 3 bedroom house knowing that other people are homeless?
How can you live your life & yet do nothing?
How can you?

How can you sleep at night?
How can you live throughout the day?
How can you work in your job?
How can you explain it to your children?
How can you live with yourself?
How can you live your life & yet do nothing?
How can you?

"The Don"
30.10.2021

Bright Eyes

(Occhi Vivaci)

Bright eyes...
... what do you see?
Bright eyes...
... what do you hear?
Bright eyes...
... what do you feel?
Bright eyes...
... what do you think?
Bright eyes...
... what do experience?
Bright eyes...
...do you see me?

Bright eyes...
...do I see what you see?
Bright eyes...
...do I hear what you hear?
Bright eyes...
...do I feel what you feel?
Bright eyes...
...do I think what you think?
Bright eyes...
...do I experience what you experience?
Bright eyes...
...do you see me?
Oh, Bright eyes.

"The Don"
30.10.2021

Religion
(Religione)

Religion...
... what is it?
Do we need it?
What's its purpose?
Yet, it's all around us.
It's thrust down our throats from the moment we are born.
We are made to believe in something.
We are in fact, FORCED to believe in something.
We are given no choice.
Some religions even say that we are born with *"Original Sin"*.
WTF!!!
I'm already a victim.
I am to blame.
I have done something wrong.
I am guilty for being born!
WOW!
This is heavy *"shit"*!
I hate religion!

WTF!
What is all this *"shit"* all about?
WTF is going on?
A religion where I have to repent for being born!
"Repent!"
"I don't know what they meant!
"Repent!"
"I don't know what they meant!
"Repent!"
"I don't know what they meant!
"Repent!"
"I don't know what they meant!

"Religion, is it the "opiate of the masses"?"

"Maybe!"

"The Don"
31.10.2021

Den of Iniquity

(Luogo dell'iniquità)

Don't smoke.
Don't drink.
Don't play your music too loud!
Don't sing!
Don't dance!
Don't have FUN!
Don't LIVE!
Only do these in your "Den of Iniquity"!

There's too much smoke!
There's too much smoking!
There's too much drink.
There's too much drinking!
There's too much loud music!
There's too much singing!
There's too much dancing!
There's too much having FUN!
There's too much LIVING!
Only do these in your "Den of Iniquity"!

My *"Den of Iniquity"* is my sanctuary.
My *"Den of Iniquity"* is my shelter.
My *"Den of Iniquity"* is my haven.
My *"Den of Iniquity"* is my world.
My "Den of Iniquity" is my paradise.
My *"Den of Iniquity"* is my HEAVEN.

Where I can...
...drink my prosecco.
...smoke my dope.
...play my music.
...sing & dance.
...do whatever the fuck I want.
I just close the doors & keep any negative energy away!
In my "Den of Iniquity".

"Would you like to visit my "Den of Iniquity"?"
"You might never want to leave".

"The Don"
31.10.2021

Born to be Wild

(Nato per essere Selvaggio)

Born to be free.
Born to express myself.
Born to be myself.
Born to be independent.
Born to be an adventurer.
Born to be curious.
Born to ask questions.
Born to be caring.
Born to be kind.
Born to be respectful.
Born to help others.
Born to be nurturing.
Born to be a rebel.
Born to be rebellious.
Born to be a Revolutionary.
I was...
...born to be wild!

Born to be wild!

"You can't tame me!"
"I was born to be wild!

"I was born to be wild!

Born to be!

"The Don"
31.10.2021

HACK THE SYSTEM

(Hackera il Sistema)

HACK THE SYSTEM.
Let's bring it down.
HACK THE SYSTEM.
Let's get into their *"mainframes"*.
HACK THE SYSTEM.
Let's sabotage their *"Information Systems"*.
HACK THE SYSTEM.
Let's get into their *"Financial Organisations"*
HACK THE SYSTEM.
Let's bring them DOWN!
HACK THE SYSTEM.
Let's bring the *"System"* DOWN!
HACK THE SYSTEM.
Let's bring it to its knees
HACK THE SYSTEM.
Let them beg for mercy.
HACK THE SYSTEM.
Let them beg for forgiveness.
HACK THE SYSTEM.
Forgiveness for their sins.
HACK THE SYSTEM.
Forgiveness for all the suffering they've caused.
HACK THE SYSTEM.
Mercy for all the unnecessary wars.
HACK THE SYSTEM.
Mercy for all the blood on their hands.
HACK THE SYSTEM.
The blood of innocent men, women & children.
HACK THE SYSTEM.
Mercy & forgiveness for all the horrendous deaths of innocent people.
HACK THE SYSTEM.
Justice has to be served.
HACK THE SYSTEM.
Their time has come!
HACK THE SYSTEM.
It's all over!

HACK THE SYSTEM.
Let's wipe away their power!
HACK THE SYSTEM.
Let's erase their money.
HACK THE SYSTEM.
Let's empty their bank accounts!
HACK THE SYSTEM.
Let's make it an *"even playing field"*!
HACK THE SYSTEM.
Let's make them live like the other 99%!

Let's hack the System!

Let's hack the System!

Let's hack the System!

Let's hack the System!

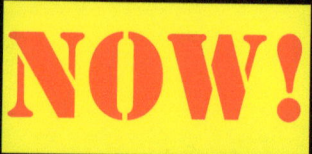

"The Don"
31.10.2021

Actions Speak Louder than Words
(Le Azioni Parlano più Forte delle Parole)

Let your actions speak for you.
You are what you did.
You are what you are doing.
You will be what you have been doing.
Because...
... actions speak louder than words.

Don't speak to me.
Don't tell me what you are about to do.
Don't tell me what you are going to do.
Don't open your mouth.
Because...
... actions speak louder than words.

Believe what I do not what I say.
Because...
... actions speak louder than words.

Let your actions speak for you!
Because...
... actions speak louder than words.

"The Don"
31.10.2021

NEVER STOP!

(Mai Smettere!)

NEVER STOP!
Never drop.
NEVER STOP!
Don't give up.
NEVER STOP!
Don't slow down.
NEVER STOP!
Don't pause.
NEVER STOP!
Don't hesitate.
NEVER STOP!
Don't procrastinate.
NEVER STOP!
Don't submit.
NEVER STOP!
Don't surrender.
NEVER STOP!
Don't quit.
NEVER STOP!

Stopping is DEATH!

NEVER STOP!

"The Don"
01.11.2021

Heaven, Hell & Earth
(Paradiso, Inferno e Terra)

There is no Hell.
There is only Heaven & Earth.
Hell is on Earth.
Deal with your Hell on Earth.

Heaven is also on Earth.
Heaven is inside us
Heaven is inside our HE♥RT.
This is Heaven & Earth.

Earth is the finite.
Heaven is the infinite.
The physical & the spiritual.
This is Heaven & Earth.

Hell, Heaven & Earth.
The *"Holy Trinity"*.
Face your Hell & you will go to Heaven.
Deal with your Hell on Earth & you will find your Heaven.

"The Don" & Miriam
02.11.2021

I Walk with Others

(Cammino con gli Altri)

I do not walk alone.
I walk with others.
I walk in solidarity with the suffering.
I belong to the *"Human Collective"*.
I do not walk alone.
I walk with others.

Shoulder to shoulder.
Hand in hand.
Body to body.
I march in protest.
I raise my voice.
I raise my open palm.
I raise my open hand.
I do not walk alone.
I walk with others.

"Do you walk with others?"
"Whom do you walk with?"
"Or, do you walk alone?"

"The Don"
02.11.2021

Which Life?

(Quale Vita?)

Is it better to live a long & boring life?
Or...
Is it better to live a short & exciting life?

Which life do you choose?

"The Don"
02.11.2021

The Men Who Sold the Earth

(Gli Uomini che hanno Venduto la Terra)

Why did they do it?
Couldn't they see the *"Climate Change Doomsday Clock"* ticking?
It's one minute to midnight.
Time is running out.
But do they care?
No!
They are...
...the men who sold the Earth.

It's Glasgow, November 2021.
World Climate Change Summit.
World leaders met.
The whole world was watching.
Greta Thunberg was there.
Sir Richard Attenborough was there.
They spoke.
Trying to convince these leaders of the industrialised nations.
To take climate change seriously.
But did they listen?
No!
They were...
...the men who sold the Earth.

It was just another *"talk fest"!*
It was just another *"wank fest"!*
It was just another photo opportunity.
It was just another opportunity to pontificate on the world's stage.
They did nothing!
They sold us out!
They shafted us again.
They sold the Earth out!
They are arseholes!
They were...
...the men who sold the Earth.

The price?
Coal & other fossil fuels!
They sold the Earth for coal!
How pathetic!
They were...
...the men who sold the Earth!

"The Don"
03.11.2021

Don't Let the Music Stop

(Non Lasciare che la Musica si Fermi)

Don't let the music die inside you.
Don't let the music die inside your head.
Don't let the music die inside your HE♥RT.
Don't let the music die inside your soul.
Don't let the music die!

Don't let the music die in your friendships.
Don't let the music die in society.
Don't let the music die in the World.
Don't let the music die inside your HE♥RT.
Don't let the music die inside your soul.
Don't let the music die!

Don't let your struggles stop the music.
Don't let your rage stop the music.
Don't let your fire stop the music.
Don't let your passion stop the music.
Don't let your LO♥E stop the music.
Don't let the music die inside your HE♥RT.
Don't let the music die inside your soul.
Don't let the music die!

"The Don"
03.11.2021

Altered Consciousness

(Coscienza alterata)

Do you seek answers?
Do you seek *altered states of mind?*
Do you seek higher *levels of consciousness?*
Do you seek the *meaning of LIFE?*
Do you seek *"The LIGHT"?*
Do you seek *"The FORCE"?*
Do you seek *"Enlightenment"?*
Do you seek *"Altered States of Consciousness"?*
Do you seek *"Altered Consciousness"?*

Do you seek *for something beyond?*
Do you seek *"UNITY"?*
Do you seek *"ONENESS"?*
Do you seek *"THE TRUTH"?*
Do you seek *"The Holy Grail"?*
Do you seek *to be one with the universe?*
Do you seek *"Altered Consciousness"?*

What do you seek?

"The Don"
03.11.2021

Reforest the Amazon!

(Rimboschire l'Amazzonia!)

Let's put it back!
Let's reforest the Amazon.

Let's seize the moment.
Let's seize the time.
Let's seize the day.
"Carpiem dium"!
We need to heal the Earth.
Now is the time.
Let's reforest the Amazon.

The lungs of the Earth are suffocating.
We need to heal them.
We need to heal the Earth.
Now is the time.
Let's reforest the Amazon.

We only have one opportunity.
We only have one chance.
This is the last chance.
We need to heal the Earth.
Now is the time.
Let's reforest the Amazon.

"The Don"
03.11.2021

Easy Prey

(Preda Facile)

You're an easy target.
You're easy game.
You're easy meat.
You're easy pickings.
You're easy prey.

If you're vulnerable.
If you're weak.
If you're troubled.
If you're not yourself.
Then...
... you're easy prey.

You stand still.
You're not curious.
You're not interested in anything.
You don't think.
You don't feel.
You're not interesting.
You're a *"soft"* target.
You're an *"easy hit"*.
You're a *"sitting duck"*.
You're easy prey.

Move.
Run.
Be fluidic.
Be adventurous.
Be a *"risk taker"*.
Be FUN.
Don't be...
...easy prey.

Are you easy prey?

"The Don"
05.11.2021

In Search for the Meaning of Life
(Alla Ricerca del Senso della Vita)

I am a wanderer.
I am a journeyman.
I am a traveller.
I am a seeker.
I am in search for the meaning of life.

I have met *Krishnamurti*.
I have met the *Dalai Lama*.
I have met Gurdjeff.
I have met *"Silo"*.
On my journey in search for the meaning of life.

I have asked questions.
I have sought our *"The Knowledge"*.
I have travelled to far off places.
I have searched for *"The Light"*.
In search for the meaning of life.

And what have I found?
What is the answer?
What is the truth?
Is there any truth to be found at all?
In my search for the meaning of life.

The simple truth that I have found I will share with you.
The answer is inside you!
Look within.
Do not seek answers outside yourself.
All the answers are inside you.
The search for the meaning of life is an internal one.

You'll be surprised at what you will find.
When you start your *"Inner Look"*.
When you journey through your *"Internal Landscape"*.
Don't be afraid.
It is what you've built.
It's who you are.
Enjoy your adventures when you go...
...in search for the meaning of life.

"The Don"
06.11.2021

Be a Warrior

(Essere un Guerriero)

Be a warrior for *respect*.
Be a warrior for *compassion*.
Be a warrior for *friendship*.
Be a warrior for *kindness*.
Be a warrior for *caring*.
Be a warrior for *human rights*.
Be a warrior for *Earth*.
Be a warrior for *Humanity*.
Be a warrior for *yourself*.

Be a warrior against *discrimination*.
Be a warrior against *prejudice*.
Be a warrior against *cruelty*.
Be a warrior against *hatred*.
Be a warrior against *exploitation*.
Be a warrior against *injustice*.
Be a warrior against *violence*.
Be a warrior against *inhumanity*.

Be a warrior!

"The Don"
06.11.2021

May All Your Dreams Come True

(Possano tutti i tuoi Sogni Avverarsi)

What do you dream of...
...a cat?
...a dog?
...friendship?
...a relationship?
...a LO♥ER?
...a house?
...a baby?
...a family?
...a just society?
...the end to wars?
...world peace?
...a sustainable future?
... overcoming your fears?
... becoming one with "Nature"?
..."The Force"?
..."The Light"?
... higher levels of consciousness?
... enlightenment?

Whatever you dream of...
...may All your dreams come true.!

"The Don"
06.11.2021

The Future

(Il Futuro)

What will our future be?
What will our future look like?
Will we be able to save the planet from climate change?
Will we be able to save the forests?
Will we be able to save the animals?
Will we be able to save humanity?
Will we be able to save ourselves?
What is the future?

Will we be able to end starvation?
Will we be able to end discrimination?
Will we be able to end exploration?
Will we be able to end injustice?
Will we be able to end hatred?
Will we be able to end violence?
Will we be able to end wars?
Will we be able to end inhumanity?
What is the future?

"The future is NOW!"

"The Don"
06.11.2021

Books written by "The Don"

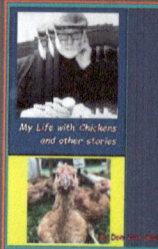

"My Life with Chickens & other stories: I Pity the Poor Immigrant"
Published:
10th September, 2019
Autobiography Book 1:
0 – 12 years old

"Poems for Misfits, Miscreants, Misanthropes, Mavericks, Losers & Malcontents!"
Published:
10th June, 2020
Book of Poems 1

"Poems for Troubled Minds & Trouble Hearts"
Published:
10th August, 2020
Book of Poems 2

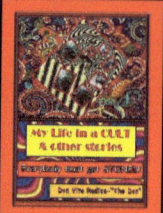

"My Life in a CULT & other stories: Everybody Must Get STONED!"
Published:
10th September, 2020
Autobiography Book 2:
15 – 30 years old

"Poems for Restless Minds & Restless Hearts"
Published:
10th October, 2020
Book of Poems 3

"Poems for Anarchists, Revolutionaries, Outlaws & Dissidents!"
Published:
10th November, 2020
Book of Poems 4

"Poems for Non-Thinkers & Eccentrics"
Published:
10th December, 2020
Book of Poems 5

"The Rantings of a Madman"
Published:
10th January, 2021
Book of Poems 6

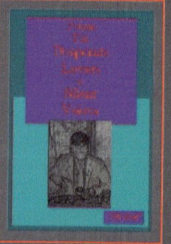

"Poems for Desperate Lovers & Silent Voices"
Published:
10th February, 2021
Book of Poems 7

"Poems for Tormented Minds & Tortured Souls"
Published:
10th March, 2021
Book of Poems 8

All available ONLY online

Books written by "The Don"

"Poems for ALIENS, Outsiders, Outcasts & other STRANGE BEINGS!"
Published: 10th April, 2021
Book of Poems 9

"Poems for Beings From Another Planet"
Published: 10th May, 2021
Book of Poems 10

"Poems for Mindless Beings & Lost Souls"
Published: 10th June, 2021
Book of Poems 11

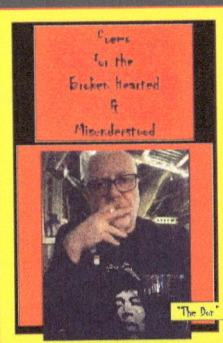

"Poems for the Broken Hearted & Misunderstood
Published: 10th July, 2021
Book of Poems 12

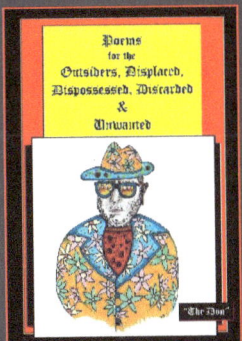

"Poems for Poems for the Bewildered, Dazed & Confused"
10th August, 2021
Book of Poems 13

"Poems for the Outsiders, Displaced, Dispossessed, Discarded & Unwanted"
Published: 10th Sept, 2021
Book of Poems 14

All available ONLY online

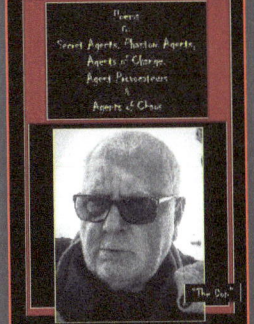

"Poems for Secret Agents, Phantom Agents, Agents of Change, Agent Provocateurs & Agents of Chaos"
Published: 10th Oct, 2021
Book of Poems 15

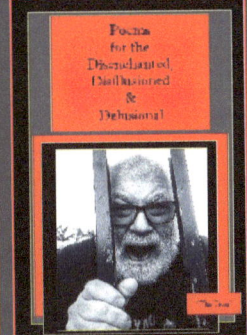

"Poems for Disenchanted, Disillusioned & Delusional
Published: 10th November, 2021
Book of Poems 16

Books written by "The Don"

"Poems for the Stoners, drugos, ACID takers & Psychedelic LO♥ERS (Everybody Must Get Stoned)"
Published: 10th December, 2021
Book of Poems 17

"Poems for Anarchists, Rebels & Revolutionaries
Published: 10th January, 2022
Book of Poems 18

"Poems for Rebels, Radicals & Revolutionaries (Viva la Révolution!)

Published: 10th February, 2022

Book of Poems 19

Vito Radice ("The Don")
(Poet/Author/Polemicist/Non-Thinker/Non-Intellectual)
Email: vitoradice@gmail.com
Instagram: don_vito_radice
Facebook: Vito Radice
Mobile: +61490012461
(Australia)

If You Can't Be with the One You LO♥E, *(LO♥E the One You're with)*
(Se non puoi Amare quello con cui Stai, (Ama quello con cui Stai))

We can't always be with the one you want, so...
...be with the one who's with you.
...be with the one who's there now.
...LO♥E the one you're with.

"The Don"
06.11.2021